Little Red Barn

Designs by Be...

Size:

Barn: 11 inches W x 10⅜ inches H x 7¼ inches D (27.9cm x 26.4cm x 18.4cm)

Horse: 6 inches L x 4¾ inches H x 1 inch D (15.2cm x 12.1cm x 2.5cm)

Pig: 4 inches L x 2⅜ inches H x ⅝ inch D (10.2cm x 6cm x 1.6cm)

Piglet: 2⅝ inches L x 1⅝ inches H x ½ inch D (6.7cm x 4.1cm x 1.3cm)

Lamb: 4¼ inches L x 2⅝ inches H x ⅝ inch D (10.8cm x 6.7cm x 1.6cm)

Hen: 2 inches L x 2⅜ inches H x ⅞ inches D (5.1cm x 6cm x 2.2cm)

Rooster: 2½ inches L x 2¾ inches H x 1 inch D (6.4cm x 7cm x 2.5cm)

Skill Level: Intermediate

Materials

❑ 6 sheets 7-count plastic canvas

❑ Red Heart Classic Art. E267 and Super Saver Art. E300 medium weight yarn as listed in color key

❑ #16 tapestry needle

❑ Size H/8/5mm crochet hook

❑ 6-inch/15.2cm-long ¼-inch (0.6cm) dowel

❑ Polyester fiberfill

Stitching Step by Step

Barn

1 Cut plastic canvas according to graphs (pages 5–9), cutting out openings in barn sides and in barn front and roof front only, leaving barn back and roof back intact. Cut one 66-hole x 40-hole piece for barn floor. Barn floor will remain unstitched.

2 Stitch and Overcast door bar and bar holders. Stitch remaining pieces following graphs. Work barn and roof back pieces, filling in entire areas with stitch pattern and colors indicated.

3 When background stitching is completed, work white Backstitches where indicated on graphs.

4 Following either step 5 or step 6, crochet or braid four handles with white.

5 Using crochet hook and leaving 4-inch (10.2cm) tails at each end, chain stitch (see illustration) until each handle measures 1½ inches (3.8cm). Fasten off. Thread tails from front to back on each Dutch door top and each side loft door where indicated on graphs; secure on back side.

Chain Stitch

6 Leaving 4-inch (10.2cm) tails at each end, braid until each handle measures 1½ inches (3.8cm). Thread tails from front to back on each Dutch door top and each side loft door where indicated on graphs; secure on back side.

Barn Assembly

1 Using white throughout, tack right side of door bar to back side of one door bar holder where indicated on graphs. Tack bar holders to barn doors where indicated on graphs.

2 Overcast barn doors, Dutch door top pieces, side loft doors and roof door, leaving edges inside brackets unworked. Overcast all openings on barn and roof pieces, leaving edges inside brackets unworked. Whipstitch doors to corresponding openings within brackets.

3 Using red throughout, Overcast top edges of sides from black dot to black dot. Whipstitch front and back to sides. Whipstitch unstitched barn floor to front, back and sides. Whipstitch front and back edges of loft floor to top edges of barn front and back; tack side edges of loft floor to sides.

4 Overcast side edges of roof handles within brackets. Whipstitch handles together along all remaining edges except bottom edges. Whipstitch bottom edges to roof top where indicated on graphs.

5 Using nickel, Whipstitch roof front and back to roof top. Overcast remaining edges with black. Center roof over barn; tack to sides with nickel.

Animals

1 Cut plastic canvas according to graphs (pages 10–13). For bellies, cut one each as follows: 21 holes by 3 holes for horse, 9 holes x 2 holes for sheep, 14 holes x 2 holes for pig, 5 holes x 1 hole for piglet. Piglet belly will remain unstitched.

2 Work Continental Stitches on bellies as follows: horse with cornmeal, sheep with white, pig with pink.

3 Following graphs, stitch and Overcast ears and wings. Stitch and Overcast hen and rooster legs and feet. Stitch sheep following graph, working Loop Stitches as shown in Loop Stitch Diagram (see illustration). Stitch all remaining pieces.

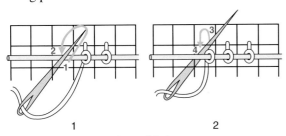

Loop Stitch
Lay dowel horizontally over canvas
Work stitches over dowel, following numbered steps
Remove dowel when row is completed

4 Work Backstitches, Straight Stitches and French Knots when background stitching is completed.

Horse Assembly

1 Overcast front and back legs on both sides from green dot to black arrow, leaving front corner with green line on each unworked.

2 Matching blue dots, tack ears to corresponding sides with cornmeal.

3 Whipstitch left and right sides together from green dot in front around head, back and tail to green dot in back. Stuff lightly with fiberfill.

4 Whipstitch front corners together where indicated with green lines. Center and Whipstitch belly to sides between arrows. Tack remaining edges of belly in place with cornmeal.

5 For mane, cut seven 4-inch (10.2cm) lengths of white yarn. Attach with Lark's Head Knots (see illustration) where indicated on graph; trim ends.

Lark's Head Knot

Sheep Assembly

1 Overcast front and back legs on both sides from green dot to black arrow.

2 Matching blue dots, tack ears to corresponding sides with white.

3 Whipstitch sides together from green dot in front around head, back and tail to green dot in back. Stuff lightly with fiberfill.

4 Center and Whipstitch belly to sides between arrows. Tack remaining edges of belly in place with white.

Pig & Piglet Assembly

1 Overcast front and back legs on both sides from green dot to black arrow.

2 Matching blue dots, tack ears to corresponding sides with pink.

3 Whipstitch pig sides together from green dot in front around head, back and tail to green dot in back. Stuff lightly with fiberfill. Repeat for piglet sides.

4 Center and Whipstitch bellies to corresponding sides between arrows. Tack remaining edges of bellies in place with pink.

Hen & Rooster Assembly

1 Tack hen wings to corresponding sides with white. Tack rooster wings to corresponding sides with warm brown.

2 Whipstitch hen sides together and rooster sides together.

3 Using orange, tack legs to feet where indicated with green lines, making two sets. Slip bottom of hen and rooster into legs where indicated with green arrows; tack in place.

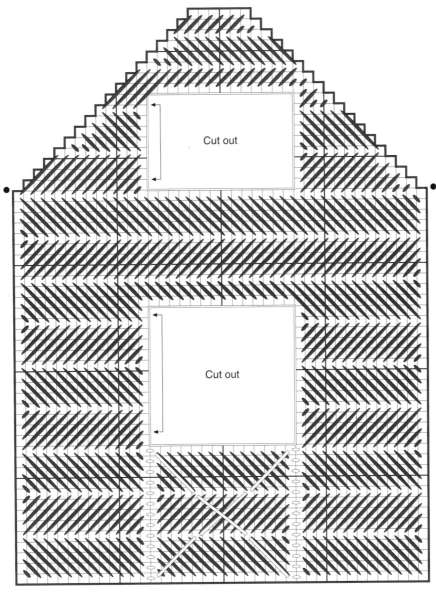

Side
40 holes x 54 holes
Cut 2

COLOR KEY
BARN

Yards	Medium Weight Yarn
200 (182.9m)	■ Cherry red #912
100 (91.5m)	▨ Nickel #401
50 (45.8m)	☐ Cornmeal #320
20 (18.3m)	☐ White #1
5 (4.6m)	⟋ Black #12 Overcast
	⟋ White #1 Backstitch and Straight Stitch
	● Attach crocheted handle
	● Attach door bar holder
	◇ Attach door bar
	● Attach roof handle

Color numbers given are for Red Heart Classic Art. E267 and Super Saver Art. E300 medium weight yarn.

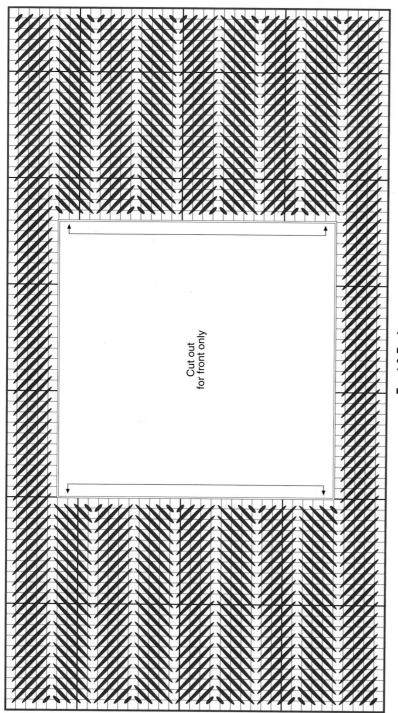

Front & Back
66 holes x 37 holes
Cut 2

Cut out
for front only

COLOR KEY
BARN

Yards		Medium Weight Yarn
200 (182.9m)	■	Cherry red #912
100 (91.5m)	▨	Nickel #401
50 (45.8m)	□	Cornmeal #320
20 (18.3m)	□	White #1
5 (4.6m)	╱	Black #12 Overcast
	⁄	White #1 Backstitch and Straight Stitch
	●	Attach crocheted handle
	●	Attach door bar holder
	◇	Attach door bar
	●	Attach roof handle

Color numbers given are for Red Heart Classic Art. E267 and Super Saver Art. E300 medium weight yarn.

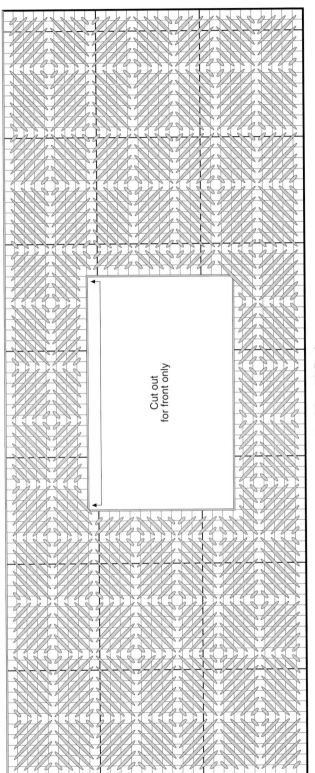

Roof Front & Back
72 holes x 29 holes
Cut 2

Cut out
for front only

Barn Roof Top
72 holes x 6 holes
Cut 1

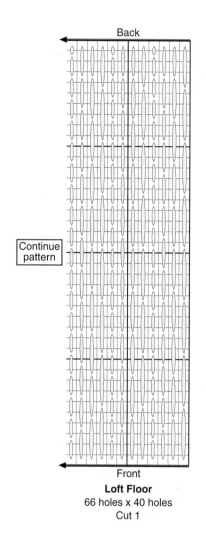

Back

Continue
pattern

Front

Loft Floor
66 holes x 40 holes
Cut 1

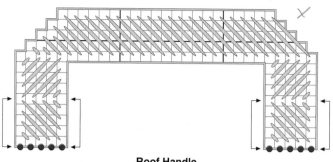

Roof Handle
29 holes x 13 holes
Cut 2

Whipstitch to roof opening

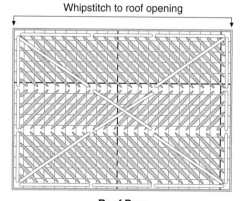

Roof Door
21 holes x 15 holes
Cut 1

COLOR KEY
BARN

Yards	Medium Weight Yarn
200 (182.9m)	■ Cherry red #912
100 (91.5m)	▨ Nickel #401
50 (45.8m)	☐ Cornmeal #320
20 (18.3m)	☐ White #1
5 (4.6m)	╱ Black #12 Overcast
	╱ White #1 Backstitch and Straight Stitch
	● Attach crocheted handle
	● Attach door bar holder
	◇ Attach door bar
	● Attach roof handle

Color numbers given are for Red Heart Classic
Art. E267 and Super Saver Art. E300 medium
weight yarn.

Barn Doors
12 holes x 25 holes each
Cut 1 set

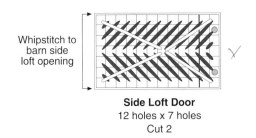

Whipstitch to
barn side
loft opening

Side Loft Door
12 holes x 7 holes
Cut 2

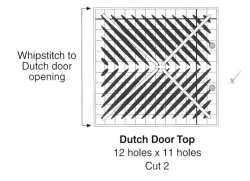

Whipstitch to
Dutch door
opening

Dutch Door Top
12 holes x 11 holes
Cut 2

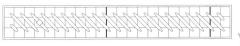

Door Bar
22 holes x 3 holes
Cut 1

Door Bar Holder
3 holes x 7 holes
Cut 2

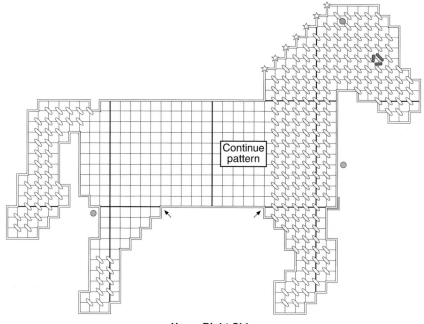

Horse Right Side
40 holes x 29 holes
Cut 1

Right   Left

Horse Ears
4 holes x 3 holes each
Cut 1 set

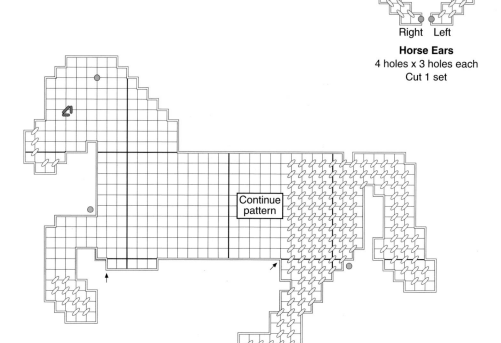

Horse Left Side
40 holes x 29 holes
Cut 1

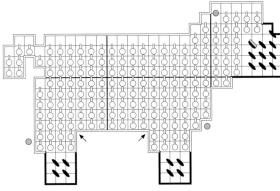

Sheep Side
27 holes x 17 holes
Cut 2, reverse 1,
reversing stitching

Right   Left

Sheep Ears
3 holes x 3 holes each
Cut 1 set

COLOR KEY ANIMALS	
Yards	**Medium Weight Yarn**
40 (36.6m)	☐ White #1
5 (4.6m)	■ Black #12
6 (5.5m)	☐ Orange #245
30 (27.5m)	☐ Cornmeal #320
10 (9.2m)	☐ Warm brown #336
25 (22.9m)	☐ Pink #737
	✎ Black #12 Backstitch
	✎ Orange #245 Backstitch
5 (4.6m)	✎ Mid brown #339 Backstitch and Overcast
1 (1m)	✎ Coffee #365 Backstitch and Overcast
1 (1m)	✎ Delft blue #885 Straight Stitch
1 (1m)	✎ Cherry red #912 Backstitch and Overcast
	● Black #12 French Knot
	⧜ White #1 Turkey Loop Stitch
	☆ White #1 Lark's Head Knot
	⬤ Attach ear
	⬤ Attach wing

Color numbers given are for Red Heart Classic Art. E267 and Super Saver Art. E300 medium weight yarn.

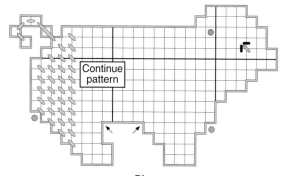

Pig
26 holes x 15 holes
Cut 2, reverse 1,
reversing stitching

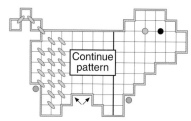

Piglet Side
17 holes x 10 holes
Cut 2, reverse 1,
reversing stitching

Right   Left

Pig Ears
3 holes x 3 holes each
Cut 1 set

Right   Left

Piglet Ears
2 holes x 2 holes each
Cut 1 set

COLOR KEY
ANIMALS

Yards	Medium Weight Yarn
40 (36.6m)	☐ White #1
5 (4.6m)	■ Black #12
6 (5.5m)	▨ Orange #245
30 (27.5m)	☐ Cornmeal #320
10 (9.2m)	☐ Warm brown #336
25 (22.9m)	☐ Pink #737
	✏ Black #12 Backstitch
	✏ Orange #245 Backstitch
5 (4.6m)	✏ Mid brown #339 Backstitch and Overcast
1 (1m)	✏ Coffee #365 Backstitch and Overcast
1 (1m)	✏ Delft blue #885 Straight Stitch
1 (1m)	✏ Cherry red #912 Backstitch and Overcast
	● Black #12 French Knot
	⬭ White #1 Turkey Loop Stitch
	☆ White #1 Lark's Head Knot
	● Attach ear
	● Attach wing

Color numbers given are for Red Heart Classic Art.
E267 and Super Saver Art. E300 medium weight yarn.

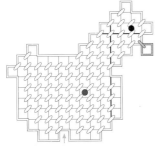

Hen Side
14 holes x 13 holes
Cut 2, reverse 1,
reversing stitching

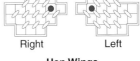

Right   Left

Hen Wings
6 holes x 4 holes each
Cut 1 set

Hen & Rooster Legs
3 holes x 3 holes
Cut 1 for each

Hen & Rooster Feet
5 holes x 6 holes
Cut 1 for each

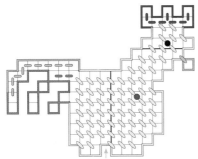

Rooster Side
18 holes x 14 holes
Cut 2, reverse 1,
reversing stitching

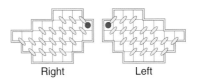

Right   Left

Rooster Wings
8 holes x 5 holes each
Cut 1 set

Dolly Bassinet

Design by Suzanne Varnell

Size: 11½ inches W x 14¾ inches L x 11 inches H
(29.2cm x 37.5cm x 27.9cm), excluding ruffle

Skill Level: Intermediate

Materials

- ❏ 4 sheets clear 7-count plastic canvas
- ❏ 4 sheets yellow 7-count plastic canvas
- ❏ Medium weight yarn as listed in color key
- ❏ #16 tapestry needle
- ❏ 24 inches (61cm) 1-inch/25mm-wide light yellow pregathered ruffle
- ❏ Hot-glue gun or hand-sewing needle and light yellow thread

Stitching Step by Step

1 Cut plastic canvas according to graphs (pages 15–17), cutting one clear and one yellow for each piece cut.

2 Stitch clear plastic canvas following graphs. Yellow plastic canvas will remain unstitched and will be used as lining or backing. Do not work Running Stitches at this time.

Assembly

1 For each hood piece, holding corners with blue dots together, and overlapping as indicated, stitch overlap down as shown on graph. Whipstitch together edges of dart behind overlap. Darts will be center top. Place unstitched hood inside stitched hood for lining. Tack together in several places.

2 For remaining pieces, place one unstitched piece behind one corresponding stitched piece so each stitched piece has a lining or backing.

3 Tack base pieces together at corners. Whipstitch handle and backing pieces together around all edges.

4 Following assembly diagram (page 18) and working through all thicknesses, Whipstitch sides together. With stitched side of base up, Whipstitch base to sides forming bassinet.

5 With back seam of hood aligned with seam of two side A pieces, Whipstitch bottom edge of hood to top edges of sides A. Overcast all remaining edges.

6 Place ends of one handle on one side B where indicated with red lines. Attach with Running Stitches where indicated. Repeat with remaining handle and side B.

7 Using hot-glue gun or hand-sewing needle and light yellow thread, attach ruffle to front edges of hood, folding ends under or trimming as desired.

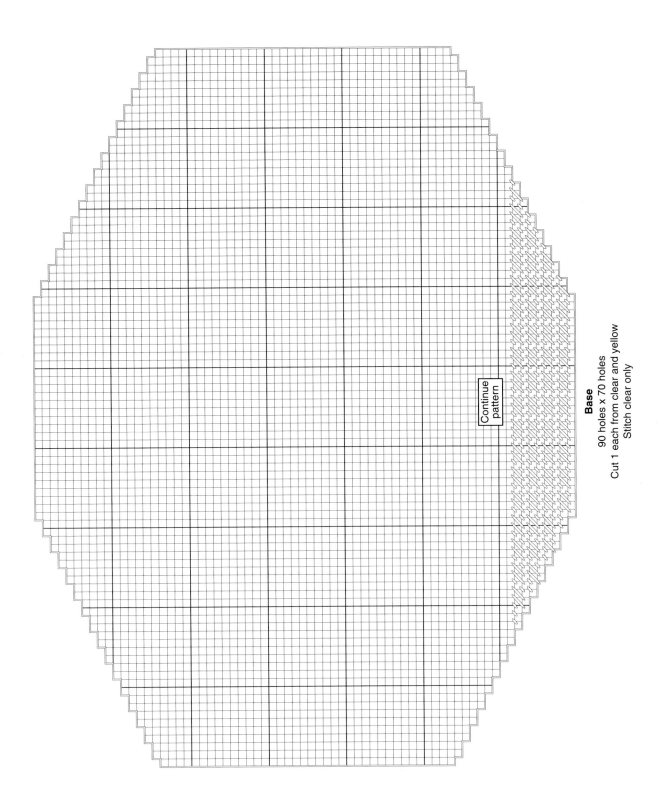

Base
90 holes x 70 holes
Cut 1 each from clear and yellow
Stitch clear only

Continue pattern

COLOR KEY	
Yards	**Medium Weight Yarn**
200 (182.9m)	☐ Light yellow
	⁄ Light yellow Running Stitch

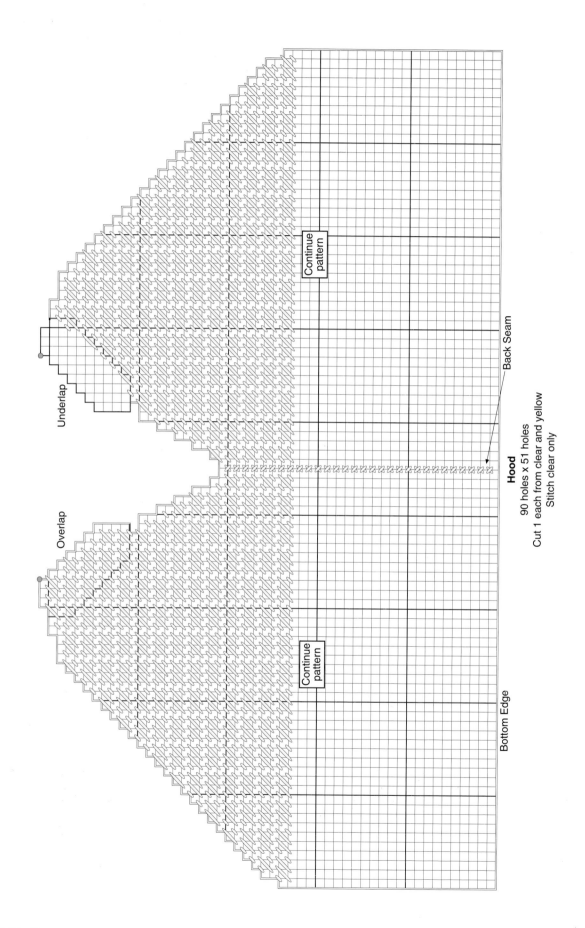

Underlap

Continue pattern

Back Seam

Hood
90 holes x 51 holes
Cut 1 each from clear and yellow
Stitch clear only

Overlap

Continue pattern

Bottom Edge

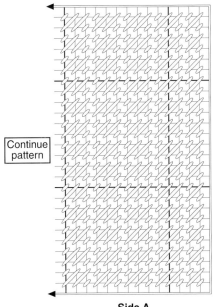

Continue pattern

Side A
54 holes x 27 holes
Cut 4 each from clear and yellow
Stitch clear only

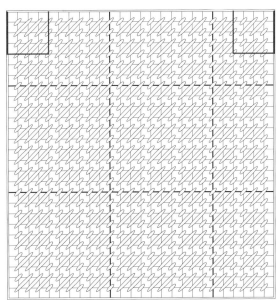

Side B
26 holes x 27 holes
Cut 2 each from clear and yellow
Stitch clear only

Continue pattern

Handle
4 holes x 89 holes
Cut 2 each from
clear and yellow
Stitch clear only

COLOR KEY	
Yards	**Medium Weight Yarn**
200 (182.9m)	☐ Light yellow
	⁄ Light yellow Running Stitch

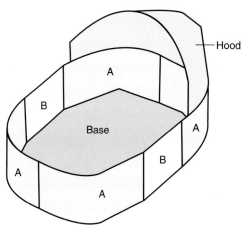

Bassinet Assembly Diagram

My Tool Playtime Set

Designs by Wilma Buckles

Size:
Toolbox 11 inches W x 5 inches H x 5 inches D (27.9cm x 12.7cm x 12.7cm)
Drill: 7¾ inches W x 6 inches H (19.7cm x 15.2cm)
Hammer: 4 inches W x 9½ inches L (10.2cm x 24.1cm)
Ruler: 13¼ inches L x 1¾ inches H (3.cm x 4.4cm)
Saw: 10¼ inches L x 4 inches H (26cm x 10.2cm)
Screwdriver: 1½ inches W x 8 inches L (3.8cm x 20.3cm)
Square: 7 inches W x 4¾ inches H (17.8cm x 12.1cm)
Wrench: 3 inches W x 5¾ inches L (7.6cm x 14.6cm)
Skill Level: Intermediate

Materials

❑ 10 sheets 7-count plastic canvas
❑ Medium weight yarn as listed in color key
❑ #16 tapestry needle

Stitching Step by Step

Toolbox

1 Cut front, back, end and handle pieces from plastic canvas according to graphs (pages 21 and 22), cutting out opening in handle pieces. Cut one 73-hole x 32-hole piece for toolbox base.

2 Stitch base with yellow Continental Stitches. Stitch remaining pieces following graphs, working uncoded areas on white background with yellow Continental Stitches unless otherwise instructed. Leave bars indicated with blue line on end pieces unworked at this time. Work one handle with green Continental Stitches as graphed and one replacing green with red.

3 Whipstitch front and back to ends, then Whipstitch front, back and ends to base. Whipstitch wrong sides of handle pieces together along inside edges, top edges from blue dot to blue dot and bottom edges from blue dot to blue dot.

4 Use a yellow Continental Stitch to Whipstitch side edges of handle pieces to end pieces at blue lines, working through all three layers.

Hammer

1 Cut hammers and hammer heads from plastic canvas according to graphs (page 23).

2 Stitch pieces following graphs, reversing one hammer and one hammer head before stitching. Work uncoded areas on white background with yellow Continental Stitches. Uncoded areas shaded in blue will remain unstitched.

3 Matching edges, Whipstitch claw ends of hammer heads to hammers from arrow to arrow. Whipstitch wrong sides of hammers and hammer heads together along remaining edges, working through all thicknesses.

Square

1 Cut squares and square handles from plastic canvas according to graphs (pages 21 and 23).

2 Stitch pieces following graphs, reversing one square before stitching. Areas shaded in blue will remain unstitched.

3 When background stitching is completed, work embroidery on handles and on square front only.

4 Whipstitch wrong sides of squares together along ruler edges. Place one square handle on each side of square over unstitched area. Whipstitch together, working through all four thicknesses and working Continental Stitches where indicated with green line.

Ruler & Saw

1 Cut plastic canvas according to graphs (page 24).

2 Stitch pieces following graphs, reversing one saw before stitching and working Continental Stitches in uncoded areas as follows: white background with yellow peach background with orange.

3 When background stitching is completed, work embroidery on ruler front pieces only.

4 Whipstitch wrong sides of saw pieces together along inside and outside edges.

5 Whipstitch ruler front pieces together between brackets. Whipstitch wrong sides of fronts and backs together. Back pieces will not be Whipstitched together so ruler will bend. If desired, Overcast adjacent edges of ruler backs.

Drill, Screwdriver & Wrench

1 Cut plastic canvas according to graphs (page 25).

2 Stitch pieces following graphs, reversing one drill before stitching and working uncoded areas on white background with yellow Continental Stitches.

3 Whipstitch wrong sides of corresponding pieces together.

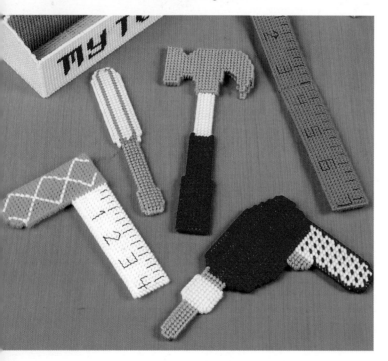

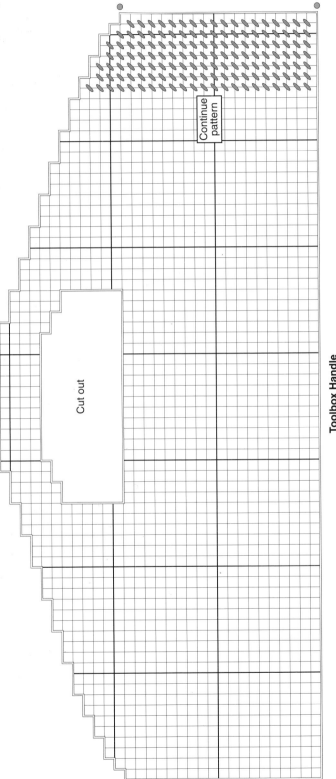

Toolbox Handle
72 holes x 31 holes
Cut 2
Stitch 1 with green as graphed
Stitch 1 replacing green with red

Cut out

Continue pattern

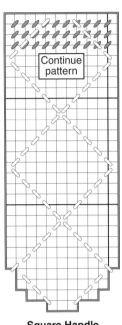

Continue pattern

Square Handle
11 holes x 28 holes
Cut 2

COLOR KEY	
Yards	**Medium Weight Yarn**
70 (64m)	■ Red
70 (64m)	■ Green
30 (27.5m)	▦ Gray
15 (13.8m)	□ White
166 (151.8m)	Uncoded areas on white background are yellow Continental Stitches
70 (64m)	Uncoded areas on peach background are orange Continental Stitches
	⁄ Yellow Overcast and Whipstitch
	⁄ Orange Whipstitch
	⁄ White Backstitch
	6-Strand Embroidery Floss
4 (3.7m)	⁄ Black (2-ply) Backstitch and Straight Stitch

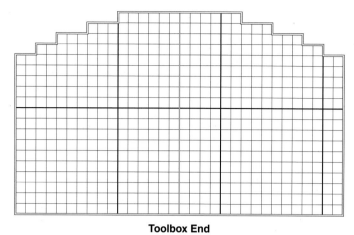

Toolbox End
32 holes x 19 holes
Cut 2

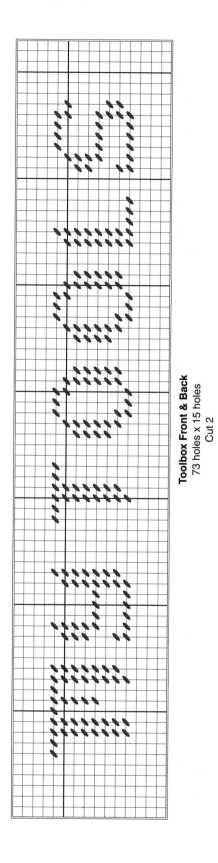

Toolbox Front & Back
73 holes x 15 holes
Cut 2

COLOR KEY

Yards	Medium Weight Yarn
70 (64m)	■ Red
70 (64m)	■ Green
30 (27.5m)	■ Gray
15 (13.8m)	□ White
166 (151.8m)	Uncoded areas on white background are yellow Continental Stitches
70 (64m)	Uncoded areas on peach background are orange Continental Stitches
	╱ Yellow Overcast and Whipstitch
	╱ Orange Whipstitch
	╱ White Backstitch
	6-Strand Embroidery Floss
4 (3.7m)	╱ Black (2-ply) Backstitch and Straight Stitch

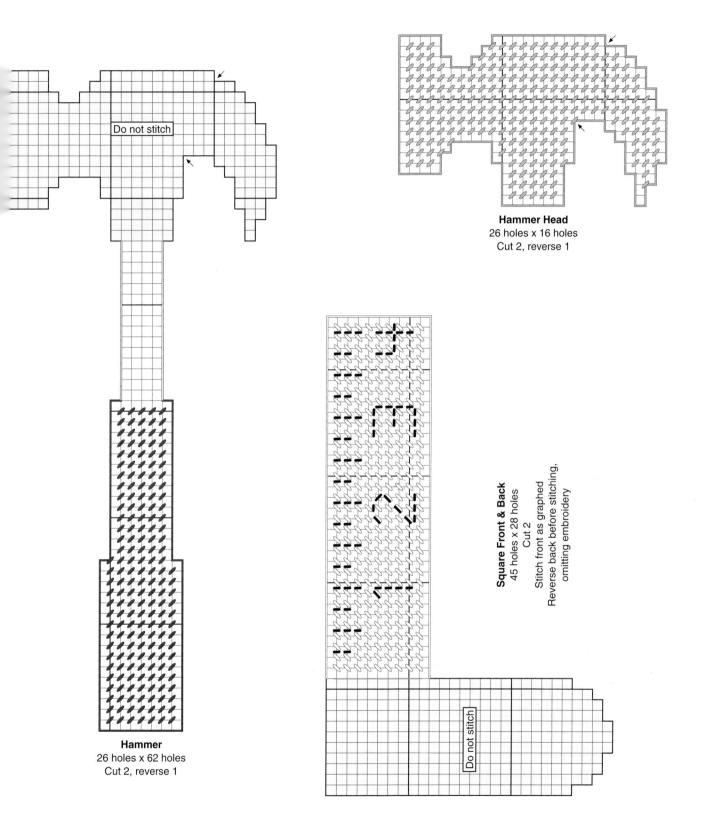

Do not stitch

Hammer Head
26 holes x 16 holes
Cut 2, reverse 1

Square Front & Back
45 holes x 28 holes
Cut 2
Stitch front as graphed
Reverse back before stitching,
omitting embroidery

Do not stitch

Hammer
26 holes x 62 holes
Cut 2, reverse 1

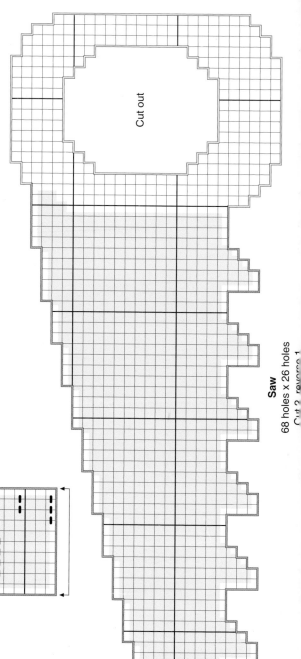

Saw
68 holes x 26 holes
Cut 2, reverse 1

Cut out

COLOR KEY

Yards	Medium Weight Yarn
70 (64m)	■ Red
70 (64m)	▨ Green
30 (27.5m)	▦ Gray
15 (13.8m)	□ White
166 (151.8m)	Uncoded areas on white background are yellow Continental Stitches
70 (64m)	Uncoded areas on peach background are orange Continental Stitches
	⁄ Yellow Overcast and Whipstitch
	⁄ Orange Whipstitch
	⁄ White Backstitch
	6-Strand Embroidery Floss
4 (3.7m)	✦ Black (2-ply) Backstitch and Straight Stitch

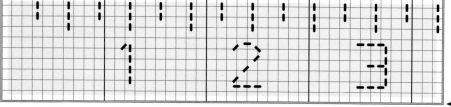

Ruler Left Side Front & Back
43 holes x 10 holes
Cut 2
Stitch front as graphed
Stitch back omitting embroidery

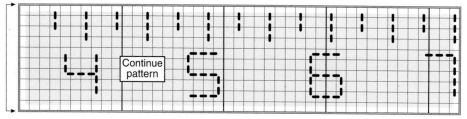

Continue pattern

Ruler Right Side Front & Back
43 holes x 10 holes
Cut 2
Stitch front as graphed
Stitch back omitting embroidery

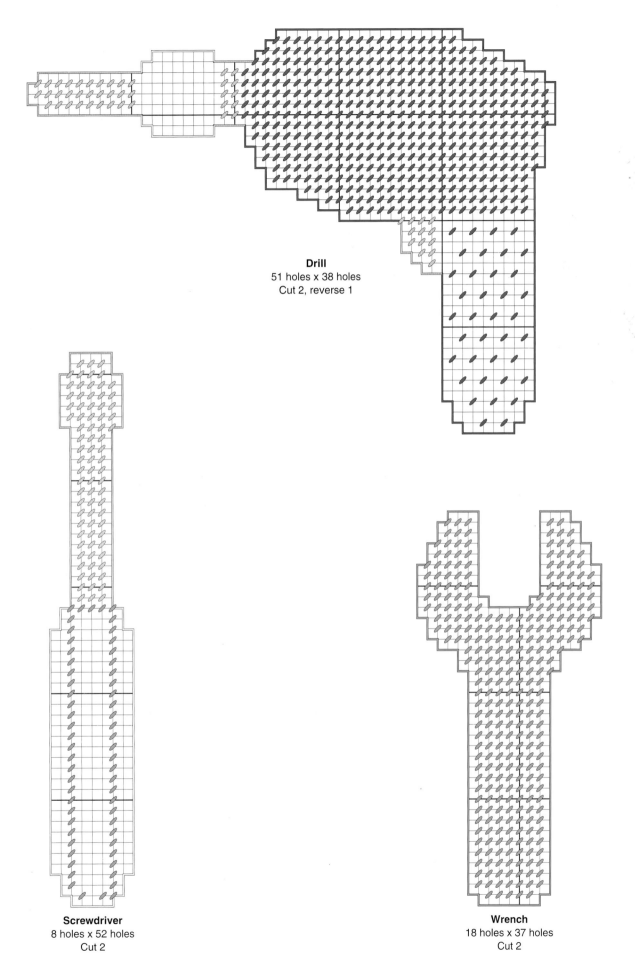

Drill
51 holes x 38 holes
Cut 2, reverse 1

Screwdriver
8 holes x 52 holes
Cut 2

Wrench
18 holes x 37 holes
Cut 2

Coloring Tote

Design by Victoria Bailey

Size: 9¾ inches W x 13⅜ inches H
(24.8cm x 34cm)

Skill Level: Intermediate

Materials

- ❏ 3 sheets 7-count plastic canvas
- ❏ Medium weight yarn as listed in color key
- ❏ #16 tapestry needle
- ❏ 4 yards (3.7m) ⅛-inch/3mm-wide white ribbon
- ❏ Craft glue or hot-glue gun

COLOR KEY	
Yards	**Medium Weight Yarn**
180 (164.6m)	☐ Light pink
10 (9.2m)	▨ Blue
10 (9.2m)	☐ Light blue
10 (9.2m)	☐ Mint green
10 (9.2m)	☐ Light yellow
10 (9.2m)	☐ Lavender
	✎ Light pink Backstitch
	⅛-Inch (3mm) Ribbon
4 (3.7m)	✎ White Straight Stitch
	⋙ Attach white ribbon bow
	● Ribbon tails

Stitching Step by Step

1 Cut plastic canvas according to graphs (pages 27–29), cutting out handle openings on back and handle.

2 Stitch pieces following graphs. Uncoded areas will remain unstitched.

3 When background stitching is completed, work white ribbon Straight Stitches on back for each balloon tie, coming up first in hole indicated with green dot, stitching around balloon as indicated, coming back up in hole with green dot, then continuing Straight Stitches as on graph. Bring ribbon up in hole indicated for ribbon tails; leaving a 2½-inch (6.4cm) tail.

4 Tie an 8-inch (20.3cm) length of ribbon in a bow and glue to back where indicated on graph.

5 Place handle on wrong side of back piece, matching edges. Whipstitch together around side and top edges from blue dot to blue dot and along inside edges. Turn back over so right side is up. Work Backstitches where indicated at bottom of handle, working through both thicknesses.

6 Overcast top edges of pockets. Place front pocket on inner pocket, aligning side and bottom edges. Whipstitch to wrong side of back along side and bottom edges. Overcast remaining edges of back.

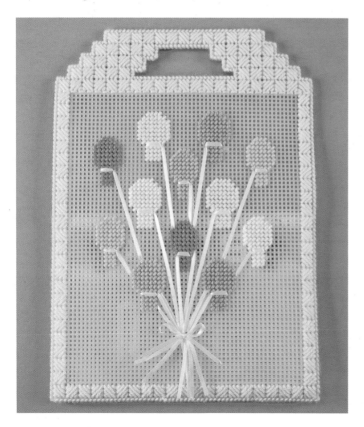

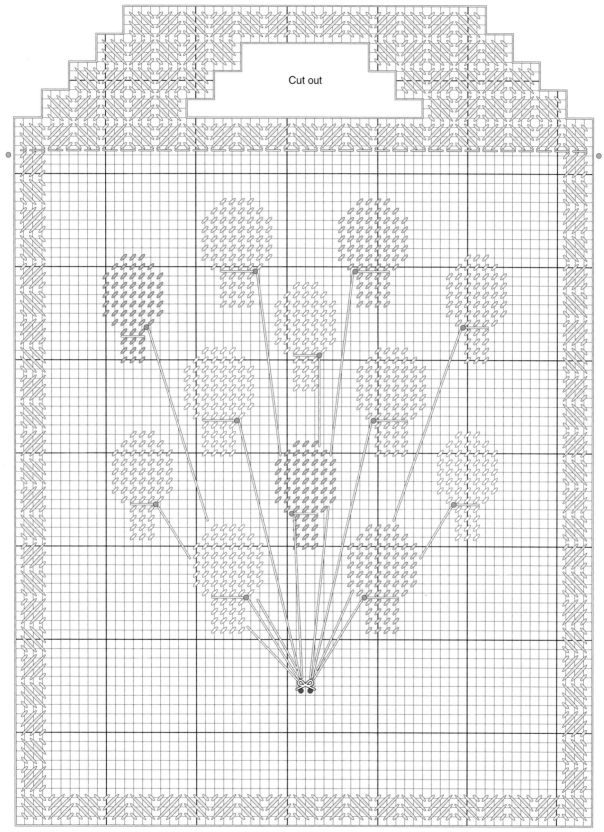

Cut out

Back
64 holes x 88 holes
Cut 1

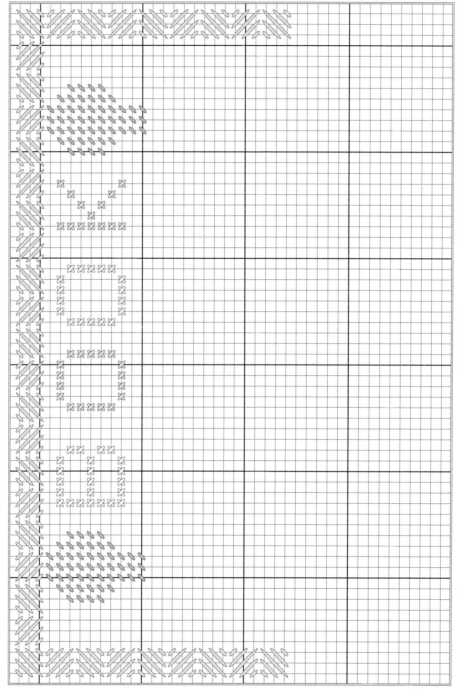

Inner Pocket
64 holes x 43 holes
Cut 1

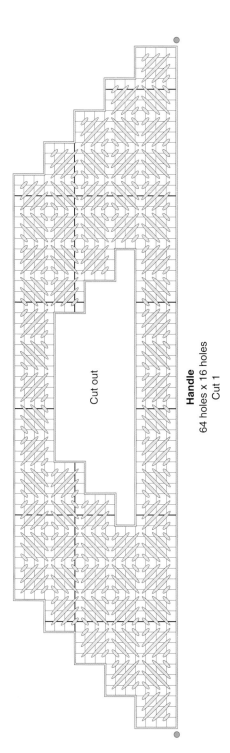

Handle
64 holes x 16 holes
Cut 1

Cut out

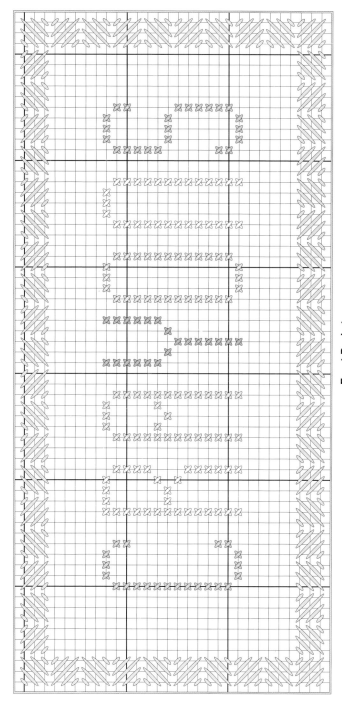

Front Pocket
64 holes x 31 holes
Cut 1

COLOR KEY	
Yards	**Medium Weight Yarn**
180 (164.6m)	☐ Light pink
10 (9.2m)	☐ Blue
10 (9.2m)	☐ Light blue
10 (9.2m)	☐ Mint green
10 (9.2m)	☐ Light yellow
10 (9.2m)	☐ Lavender
	⁄ Light pink Backstitch
	¹⁄₈-Inch (3mm) Ribbon
4 (3.7m)	⁄ White Straight Stitch
	⧓ Attach white ribbon bow
	● Ribbon tails

Going Places

Designs by Judy Blok

Size: **Box:** 3¾ inches W x 5¼ inches H x
3⅛ inches D (9.5cm x 13.3cm x 7.9cm),
including handle
Road & Runway 10½ inches W x
35¾ inches L (26.7cm x 90.8cm), unfolded;
10½ inches W x 17⅞ inches L
(26.7cm x 45.4cm), folded

Skill Level: Intermediate

Materials

- ❑ 5 sheets 7-count plastic canvas
- ❑ Medium weight yarn as listed in color key
- ❑ #16 tapestry needle
- ❑ Miniature toy cars and planes
- ❑ Craft glue or hot-glue gun

Stitching Step by Step

1 Cut plastic canvas according to graphs (pages 32–39), cutting out door openings on house, garage and small hanger front pieces only, leaving back pieces intact. Cut one 34-hole x 19-hole piece for box base. Box base will remain unstitched.

2 Overcast terminal tower antenna with white. Stitch garage, house and small hanger front pieces following graphs. Work back pieces, filling in entire area with Continental Stitches in colors indicated.

3 Stitch remaining pieces following graphs, working Continental Stitches in uncoded areas as follows: white background with black, gray background with gray, blue background with blue and yellow background with medium yellow. Do not stitch bars indicated with brown, pink, red, blue, orange and purple lines. Do not stitch center area of terminal roof as indicated.

4 When background stitching is completed, wor[k] Running Stitches, Backstitches and French Knots.

Base Assembly

1 Whipstitch one base handle each to bottom edge of base A and top edge of base B, extending roa[d] runway.

2 Whipstitch top edge of base A to bottom edge o[f] base B. Overcast all remaining edges.

House, Garage & Small Hanger Assembly

1 For garage and house, Whipstitch sides t[o] corresponding front and back pieces. Overcast to[p] edges and garage door openings.

2 Using green throughout, Whipstitch bottom edge[s] of garage to base A where indicated with blu[e] lines. Whipstitch bottom edges of house to base A wher[e] indicated with red lines.

3 Using black, Whipstitch small hanger front and bac[k] to small hanger top/side, easing as necessary to fi[t]. Overcast door opening on front.

4 Using green, Whipstitch small hanger to base [A] where indicated with purple lines.

4 Overcast terminal and tower roofs. Whipstitch tower front and back to tower sides; Overcast top edges. Using white, Whipstitch bottom edges to bars indicated with red lines on terminal roof.

5 Using white, tack antenna to tower roof where indicated on graph.

6 Center and glue terminal roof to terminal. Center and glue tower roof to tower.

Large Hanger & Terminal Assembly

1 For large hanger, using black throughout, Whipstitch back to top/side, easing as necessary to fit. Whipstitch front to top/side between arrows. Using gray, Continental Stitch remaining edges of top/side, to bars with brown lines on front.

2 Using green, Whipstitch large hanger to base B where indicated with orange lines.

3 For terminal, Whipstitch sides to front and back with blue gray; Overcast top edges. Using green, Whipstitch to base B where indicated with pink lines.

Planes & Cars Box

1 Whipstitch box front and back to box sides. Whipstitch front, back and sides to unstitched base. Overcast top edges of sides only.

2 Whipstitch bottom edges of box flaps to top edges of front and back. Whipstitch handles to flaps between arrows. Overcast all remaining edges.

3 Fold flaps in, keeping handles up.

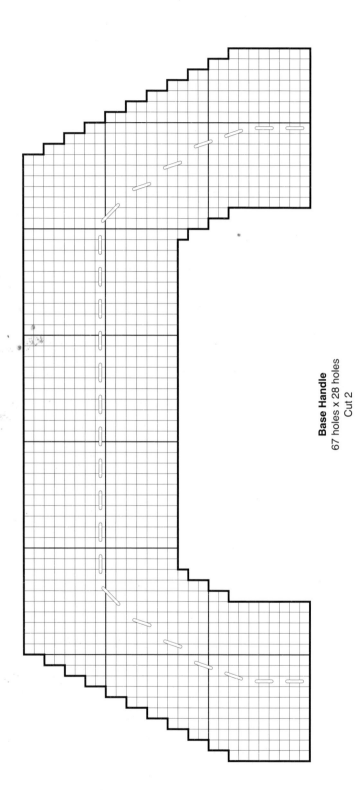

Base Handle
67 holes x 28 holes
Cut 2

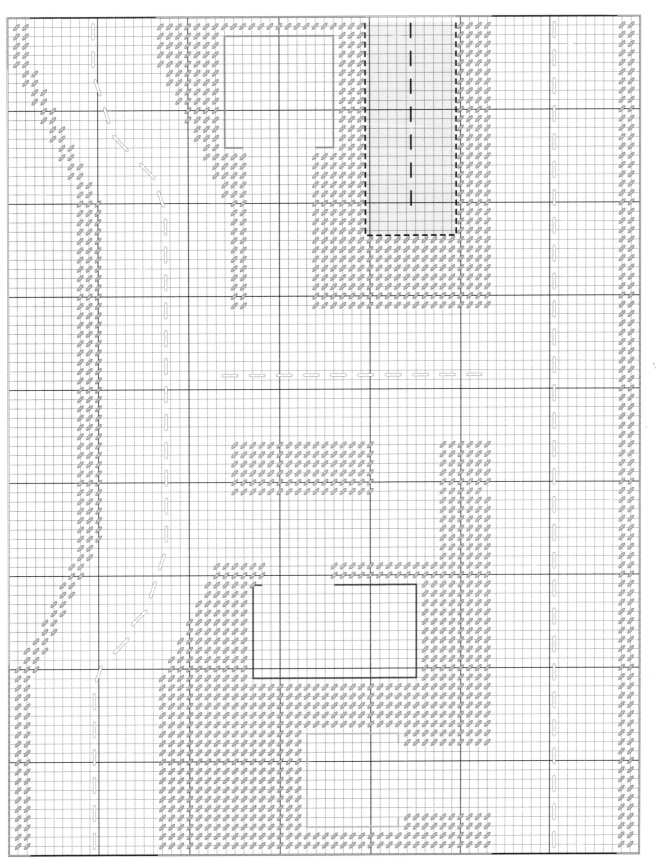

Base A
70 holes x 90 holes
Stitch 1

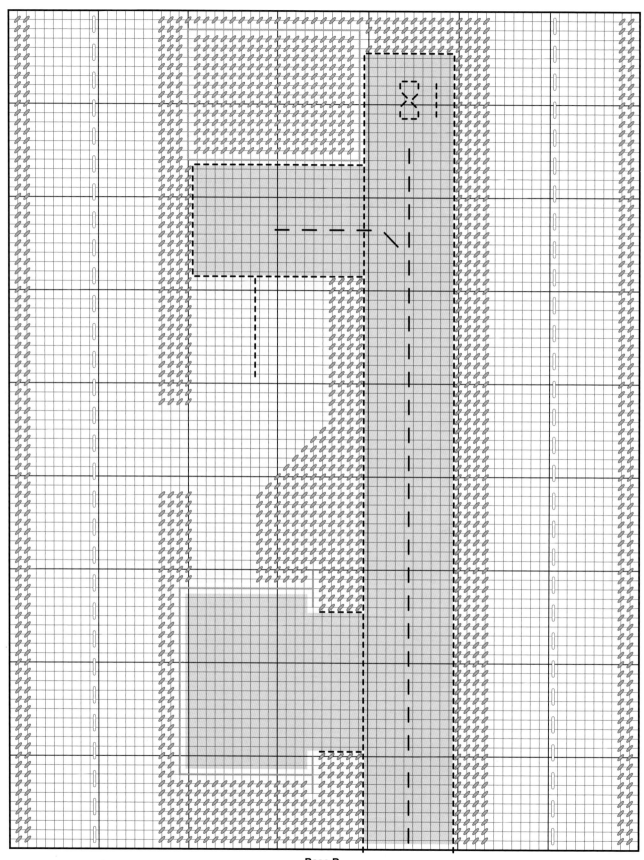

Base B
70 holes x 90 holes
Stitch 1

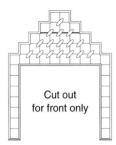

Garage Front & Back
10 holes x 12 holes
Cut 2

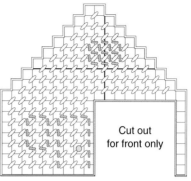

House Front & Back
18 holes x 16 holes
Cut 2

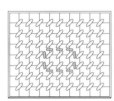

Garage Side
10 holes x 8 holes
Cut 2

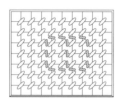

House Side
10 holes x 8 holes
Cut 2

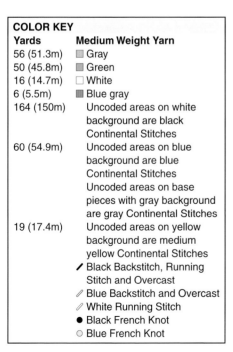

COLOR KEY	
Yards	**Medium Weight Yarn**
56 (51.3m)	▨ Gray
50 (45.8m)	▨ Green
16 (14.7m)	☐ White
6 (5.5m)	▨ Blue gray
164 (150m)	Uncoded areas on white background are black Continental Stitches
60 (54.9m)	Uncoded areas on blue background are blue Continental Stitches
	Uncoded areas on base pieces with gray background are gray Continental Stitches
19 (17.4m)	Uncoded areas on yellow background are medium yellow Continental Stitches
	✏ Black Backstitch, Running Stitch and Overcast
	✏ Blue Backstitch and Overcast
	✏ White Running Stitch
	● Black French Knot
	○ Blue French Knot

Top Edge

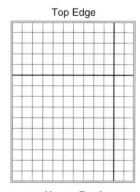

House Roof
12 holes x 15 holes
Cut 2

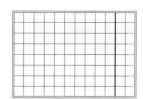

Garage Roof
12 holes x 8 holes
Cut 2

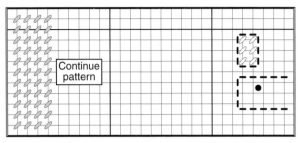

Small Hanger Top/Side
28 holes x 12 holes
Cut 1

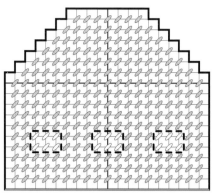

Large Hanger Back
20 holes x 17 holes
Cut 1

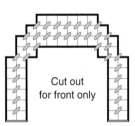

Cut out
for front only

Small Hanger Front & Back
12 holes x 10 holes
Cut 2

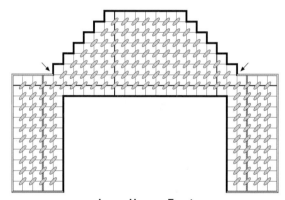

Large Hanger Front
26 holes x 17 holes
Cut 1

Back Edge

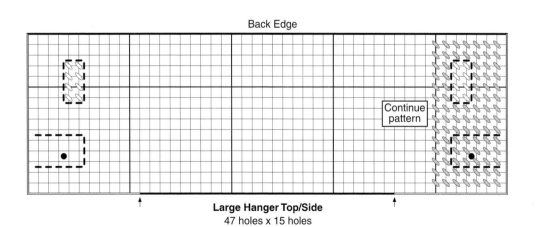

Large Hanger Top/Side
47 holes x 15 holes
Cut 1

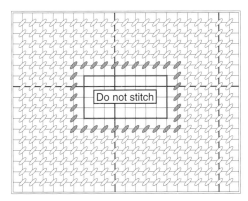

Terminal Roof
22 holes x 17 holes
Cut 1

**Terminal Tower
Front & Back**
8 holes x 6 holes
Cut 2

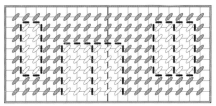

Terminal Front & Back
20 holes x 9 holes
Cut 2

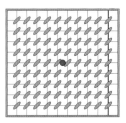

Terminal Tower Roof
11 holes x 10 holes
Cut 1

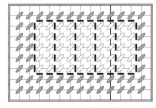

Terminal Side
14 holes x 9 holes
Cut 2

Terminal Tower Side
8 holes x 6 holes
Cut 2

Terminal Tower Antenna
5 holes x 3 holes
Cut 1

COLOR KEY	
Yards	**Medium Weight Yarn**
56 (51.3m)	Gray
50 (45.8m)	Green
16 (14.7m)	White
6 (5.5m)	Blue gray
164 (150m)	Uncoded areas on white background are black Continental Stitches
60 (54.9m)	Uncoded areas on blue background are blue Continental Stitches
	Uncoded areas on base pieces with gray background are gray Continental Stitches
19 (17.4m)	Uncoded areas on yellow background are medium yellow Continental Stitches
✦	Black Backstitch, Running Stitch and Overcast
╱	Blue Backstitch and Overcast
╱	White Running Stitch
●	Black French Knot
○	Blue French Knot

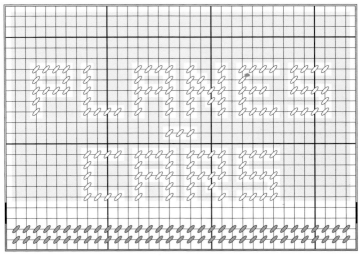

Box Front & Back
34 holes x 23 holes
Cut 2

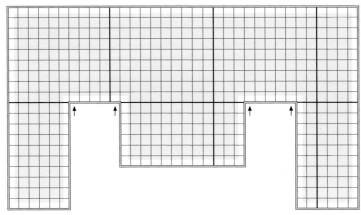

Box Top Flap
34 holes x 19 holes
Cut 1

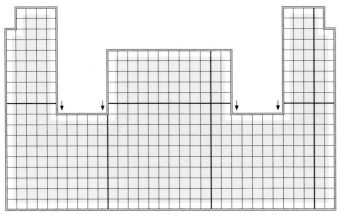

Box Bottom Flap
32 holes x 19 holes
Cut 1

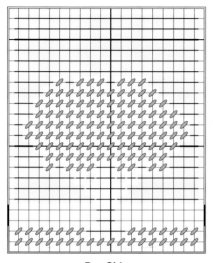

Box Side
19 holes x 23 holes
Cut 2

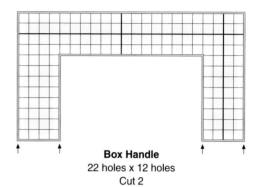

Box Handle
22 holes x 12 holes
Cut 2

COLOR KEY

Yards	Medium Weight Yarn
56 (51.3m)	Gray
50 (45.8m)	Green
16 (14.7m)	White
6 (5.5m)	Blue gray
164 (150m)	Uncoded areas on white background are black Continental Stitches
60 (54.9m)	Uncoded areas on blue background are blue Continental Stitches
	Uncoded areas on base pieces with gray background are gray Continental Stitches
19 (17.4m)	Uncoded areas on yellow background are medium yellow Continental Stitches
	∕ Black Backstitch, Running Stitch and Overcast
	∕ Blue Backstitch and Overcast
	∕ White Running Stitch
	● Black French Knot
	○ Blue French Knot

Annie's Attic®

ISBN: 978-1-59635-358-9

Printed in USA

1 2 3 4 5 6 7 8 9

Getting Started

Before You Cut

Buy one brand of canvas for each entire project as brands can differ slightly in the distance between bars. Count holes carefully from the graph before you cut, using the bolder lines that show each 10 holes. These 10-count lines begin from the left side for vertical lines and from the bottom for horizontal lines. Mark canvas before cutting; then remove all marks completely before stitching. If the piece is cut in a rectangular or square shape and is either not worked, or worked with only one color and one type of stitch, the graph is not included in the pattern. Instead, the cutting and stitching instructions are given in the general instructions or with the individual project instructions.

Covering the Canvas

Bring needle up from back of work, leaving a short length of yarn on back of canvas; work over short length to secure. To end a thread, weave needle and thread through the wrong side of your last few stitches; clip. Follow the numbers on the small graphs beside each stitch illustration; bring your needle up from the back of the work on odd numbers and down through the front of the work on even numbers. Work embroidery stitches last, after the canvas has been completely covered by the needlepoint stitches.

Shopping for Supplies

For supplies, first shop your local craft and needlework stores. Some supplies may be found in fabric, hardware and discount stores. If you are unable to find the supplies you need, please visit anniesattic.com.

Basic Stitches

Continental

Overcast

Whipstitch

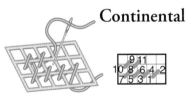

Slanted Gobelin

Long

Cross

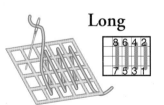

Embroidery Stitches

French Knot

Lazy Daisy

Backstitch

Straight

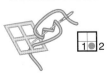
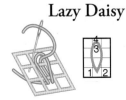

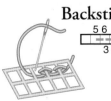

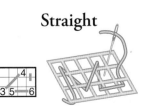

METRIC KEY:
millimeters = (mm)
centimeters = (cm)
meters = (m)
grams = (g)